ACHING FOR THE AMEN
a long poem
by Dannielle E. Carr

ACHING FOR THE AMEN

A LONG POEM

Dannielle E. Carr

P

Passengers Press 2022

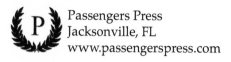
Passengers Press
Jacksonville, FL
www.passengerspress.com

Carr, Dannielle E.
1st edition.
ISBN: 978-0-578-28628-0

Manuscript Editor: Kimberly Casey
Press Editor-in-Chief: Zac Furlough

Cover design and book layout: Andreea Ceplinschi

To our girls, Eva and Amelia

all shall be well
and all shall be well
and all manner of thing
shall be well [1]

1   Jesus' words to Julian of Norwich, medieval anchoress, as recorded in her book, Revelations of Divine Love, "The Thirteenth Revelation: Chapter XXVII"

do you see, lord?

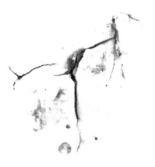

you must see.

him, as a child, squishing chicken intestines
between his fingers

you must see
him, helping his grandmother
blanch, pluck, debowel and sell them, right?

you must see.

did you see, then?
them, those surgeons
squishing his mutated inwards parts

you did see.

them, those sheathed hands
eager to debulk tumors glistening with life

you did see.

them, those tumors suffocating
his passageways

you did see.

if only you, god, would slay
the wicked. away from him

you who are bloodthirsty. he is overrun
malignant parasites won't stop

feeding, growing until he is dead.
do you remember creating

his inmost being? you do
knitting him together in his mother's womb?

you must. he brims
with tetris pharmacodynamics

celecoxib substituted for celebrex
this is a white, oblong-shaped tablet imprinted

gabapentin, common brand neurontin
take one capsule by mouth 3 times a day

how else is he supposed to take
a capsule? his rectum is on fire

ondansetron, common brand zofran
this is a yellow, oval-shaped tablet imprinted

zolpidem tartrate substituted for ambien
this is a pink, round-shaped tablet imprinted

enoxaparin sodium single dose syringes
for subcutaneous injection

capecitabine/fluorouracil/irinotecan
and bevacizumab with neulasta

do you not see, lord?

thou shalt not be tempested
thou shalt not be travailed
thou shalt not be [dis-eased]
thou shalt not be overcome [2]

---

2 Julian of Norwich, Revelations of Divine Love, "The Sixteenth Revelation: Chapter LXVIII"

finger skin
thick, rough over
me, i'll take it—
crusted layers
separate from

what used to be
youth, subsumed
under cracked purlicue

stripping eponychia
need oil for relief, but
i'll take it, lord knows
the thick

unpeeled, flaking skin
cannot be shed

        peel it, peel yourself
        cut it, cut yourself

        leave it or bite it
        thick

        nothing to do
        except oil and prayer

                what is transgression?
                wrist thick with flesh

                veins, muscle, nerves
                tendons pierced

                rust
                the punisher's sweat

                the space between pulse
                and ever, pierced

sometimes i forget the way
sickness is supposed to be

pare failing organs   with
hope
for clean margins

                                                              so, this liver

resection

                                        doesn't sound so bad

marred in the hand
he made it again [3]

                    peri-
                tonect-
                    omy

                                    with hyper-

                                                    thermic intra-
                                                            peri-
                                                        ton e al
                                                    chemotherapy

miracles happen

                                            sigmoidectomy:
                        laparoscopic sigmoidectomy for
                                diverticulitis: a prospective
study

                        (what does this have to do with
                            anything) people also google
                                what is a sigmoid colon
                            resection how long does it take
                            to recover from sigmoid colon
                            resection how long does it take
                                to do a sigmoidoscopy
                            what is the hartmann's pouch
                            (learn something every day)
                            what is a sigmoid tumor what
                                is resection of the colon
                                        (here we go)

───────────────
3   Jeremiah 18:4 (NKJV)

hope for when
                        port-a-cath port-a-potty (port-au-prince)
human devastation
cannot forget
                   incisions   intersect at the navel
life-drone
long shower ceiling fan computer fan dishwasher sleep
mull over memory   while inside is inflamed
while living

i can't go on like this

that's what you think
someone in me said

fleeced of youth fleeced fleecing stomach lining
flaming frenulum dry tongue clapping milky saliva paste

cast(e) cyst -emology

long walk to freedom, huh, rolihlahla[4] la la
lull us, us free dumb song long sufferers crossing

over a long stitch together apart apart apart
historio- carto- graphic-longing watching mds scrawl

on paper scrap crap lap walk run past
pant die megaphone research die

colorectal survival   *no data*[5]

out the naked window

dive dive dive sono- graphic-brain ex-
implosion implausible imp inky dinky

say, hyperlinked hissy fit harangue
habakkuk one two sheep weep wept

jesus

molten metal bell foundry
folly fancy or -ful faithful as robed footfall

wage war on licit drugs like leaf falls
fresh on us without custody of faculty

fecund feral found in the thicket
once more ear to vibrations in the sand

---

4   Rolihlahla was Nelson Mandela's birth name, given by his father.
5   There were no survival testimonies for Colorectal Cancer on the cancer
     treatment center's website.

21

hugging moons chasing mo' better blues
i will love you today weigh the sand

inveigh

preacher prone to wander about the sound
of rain | | || | |||| |||| |||| ||||||| |||||||||||||

un-drop un-absorb un-feel jade pastures
un-casket un-balm un-whisper so sorry

butterflies have no boundaries
soft esophagus erupts with acid

bashfulness doesn't suit a person in need

he smiled, bare-chested
—inhale—
punctured

impression history technique
impression history technique
impression history technique
impression history technique
impression history technique
impression history technique
impression history technique
impression history technique
impression history technique
impression history technique
impression history technique
impression history technique
impression history technique
impression history technique
impression history technique
impression history technique
impression history technique
impression history technique
impression history technique

impression

        no evidence of metastatic disease in the chest

        stable subcentimeter hypodense lesion

        sigmoid resection stable status

        post left hepatic lobe lateral segmentectomy

history

        response to treatment

        restaging (march 2010) malignant neoplasm of colon

technique

        unenhanced images of the liver

        obtained at 5 mm interval and thickness

        all scans were reviewed at various window settings

        study is compared with last ct scan 8/19/2017

                                                            is he well?
how much longer   /   does he have to continue chemo?

doc   /   honey   /   are you happy?
god is good, right?   /   god you are good, right?

                          the greatest disease in the west today is not tb or leprosy
                                                            is it cancer?
                              it is being unwanted, unloved and uncared for

                              we can cure physical diseases with medicine
we can   /   can we?
                  but the only cure for loneliness, despair and hopelessness is love

love of   /   for god /   another kind?
there are many in the world who are dying for a piece of bread but there are many more dying

                                              for a little love[6]
                              suggestion to change to a lot

---

6   Edited popular quotes from Mother Theresa, whose life served the poorest
     of the poor.

there's a hunger

you must see

we can't go back
through the canyon
carried away like silt
in a river, hard to know
where we came from, how
current overwhelmed particles
against rocks struck over
over and eroded for generations

look,

a spirit standing on the bank
wondering akimbo, now rowing
a raft downstream with us, even
towards children playing in the shallow
where frigid river, warm sea folded over
gaps in memory closed taut like skin graft

don't waste my pain

my love said
more blood in the bowl than anything else

human-made emissions
stinking to high heaven

jesus said
get up, take your mat

no chance
thirty percent
—   more acidity in the ocean's neck
—   live for up to five years, no more

sit and weep and remember
river stones dig soles

i don't curse, but i want to

remember his face was the moon
alight with pockets of frustration and refrain

from afar i saw his blue-eyed deliverance
by the window, round

jazz notes swung down the banister
while i dreamed in the almond tree

overrun with red ants
he sat, away, and i loved

the fall between the ground and leaves
i could not reach

god is gold
layers of metal brick and marrow

to build a tower that will not be struck
down to confusion like jesus to earth

shining in unexpected margins
joining hands with the sick

the heart of the sun
is to cleanse the wound, of course

stinging, forming a scab over
what was freshly bare

my soul can take it
god knows

he rocks the leaves
without force, some days

my father said all our joy
is touched with pain

i receive only what i have been given
an endless rain along heaven's euphrates

sit and weep and remember
by the river lapping feet that forget

in falling and in rising
we are ever preciously kept
in one love [7]

go back to sleep

7   Julian of Norwich, Revelations of Divine Love, "Chapter LXXXII"

some miracles take time

such silence. life's disquiet pacified
and winters wrought to bring destruction, calmed

to help a heart replete with agitation
and wild regrets recoil to dormancy

a butterfly can hold nothing. no hope
for long tomorrows, except in migration

but first dark, heated, pressured, coiled membranes
purposed for flight refuse to release peace

to leave the world alone while healing comes
requires resolve to be unmoved by meanness

then sunlight, spontaneous flourishing
erupting, spreading wings casting pollen

over the threadbare joy that almost ceased
to hum within swarming resilience

i used to sit on a ledge
close to the ground, watch
blades shake, brown grass-
hoppers and jumping spiders.

i used to follow biting ants
along their slow-marching slog to an unknown tuft
end and unannounced, turn back.

i used to wave at planes
like sky mowers shaving
me down to size, i
used to carve shapes out of clouds, make
stories of what they will be
truly, i tell you—

i used to twirl unhindered.

they sit in yellowing water
by the windowsill
frilled faces towards the sun
beams through blinds
they're still wrapped
in plastic, gathered, waiting
to be pruned for bathroom guests

      i, too, have been sitting
      unable to find troubled water
      i need a hand

            he needs

                it won't

                    stay in his stomach
                      or even his neck

                      over the bowl
                      or sink he bends

                  out comes sautéed shrimp
                      or peanuts and iceream

                      food is fraud
                  or his body the enemy

                  that will not even go to
                      or stay asleep

                  coyotes yapping
            or dogs, sirens, crickets, regrets

                      breaths
                  breaths
        and breaths
        of the sound

        asleep

chi chi bud oh!

some a dem a holla
some a bawl

some a[8]

> quail, punctuated headdress
> bathe in dirt
> sprint on air
> fly like a whistle away
> from danger, together
> who cries, then?
> the wounded

---

8   A flock of birds. From Jamaican folklore popularized by Jamaican Cultural
     Icon, Louise Bennett-Coverley or affectionately, Miss Lou.

39

remember when you had
a sense of humor
my love said

remember when you were
kind

pray with a child
by rote and giggles

sing a chorus, try to
mean what you say

she cracks an eye
bares some teeth

kneels high on a chair
above the breakfast table

buries her face at night
deep in a pillow so

jesus becomes, to me
fleetings and rainbows

who slips past lips
to forehead, past

hands to meals
past sleep to sunrise

and smog, the earth
is real, jesus is

play and longing

at the end, please
our lips from sin
our hearts from shame[9]
his nodes from cancer

what an ugliness in the world

---

9   Part of a verse from the hymn, "Savior, Again to Thy Dear Name" sung as
     the Recessional at the Anglican church I attended as a child.

like a dog
grass can be tamed
but not growth

fingernails
nose hairs, cancer
cells corrupt

ms. angelou,

> now i understand

my grandpa's laugh

> that easy chuckle

was not what i thought

> with that shaking, bobbing head baring teeth, graying the soul

it was a mask, *that survival apparatus*

> yes, his mouths were *myriad subtleties*[10]

scoffing at his sold soul

> horrifying, beneath lovely in memory

---

10   Quotes from Maya Angelou's introduction to and reading of her compilation
of Paul Lawrence-Dunbar's "Wear the Mask" and her poem "For Old Black
Men" at a conference called, "Facing Evil" in central Texas.

All things are wearisome,
more than one can say.[11]

---

now tissue shaped by sound
transmitted by lubricated probe—
an intimate tool echoes
our desires minus eros equals
follicles, floating dark
holes of potential

now sweet belly growth
and sour saliva are borne
in my healthy body
which carries no matter
how much i try put off
his chemo slump at ob visits
acid spit ups, or call out
to heaven. weight comes
back to burden my face
with moods, press slouched
shoulders away from god, him
myself—wrapped around
an innocent flourishing
despite

an orchid's green leaf
is plastic countenance
waxed over

i do not care/know how
to care for it
how do i know
if it lives

angry god

god-angry

wounded god

god-wounded

with holes in

hands i wish

could hold me

you, god

lingered

until there was death
to shout *lazarus, come out!*

will you find faith on earth
in me? i do not know
how much i'll have to give
my lord, how much i'll have to try
to look with all my heart for just one
faithful
part of
me

morning comes in slatted darkness
a slow creeping of the day
keeps a deaf blind numb sleep
in the body, dreaming
of no-name neighbors
who keep coming back to ask, to sing
are you alright

this finch looks at me, fierce
ruffled in disdain for my complaints
after what it is after, always
until its body says, enough.

    i'm in its way. it won't stand
    on legs i could break without effort
    for whatever i feel powerless to pursue.
    i stare. it swoops low against

        the air i won't master around me.
        it cannot move me from this low
        point. it cannot move me
        though, by god, it tries.

i saw a bearded, sunburned son of man
rifling through the garbage

i walked past, carrying mine
to the car. i turned back to offer

money, food, whatever he needed
as if i could supply or mend

he refused me, with gentleness, asked
are you alright

no.

o lilting shadows of peppercorn leaves
your peace misleads my fear
that is not misplaced.
when i leave this plastic wicker chair
will you search for me again
in the cool of the day?

god gifts me, sullen, with sound
in the ear, monochrome imagination
for what has never been seen
except on scritta, and only if read
and only if understood, and if only
i really knew what to tell you

i will approach the afternoon
(because the morning has passed)
with god by my side, or
leaning against the mildewed wall, or
sitting on the rock, beside
a bronzed frog, reclining, or
behind my ribcage, because i hear
a voice telling stories that can't find
a place to be of good use

i wish i felt

not so low

muted behind
persian cucumbers
cut and sprinkled
with tahín on the tongue

click of a gas stove pilot
pots banging against soft
tissue beneath my skull
fluid draining to the sewerage

shades of green, shapeless growth
against a blue haze, gray machinery
never stops passing, filling empty

what if i were to pray

god would not be closer

the haunt his body holds. it frightens me. the haunt his body holds. it
frightens me. the haunt his body holds. it frightens me. the haunt his
body holds. it frightens me. the haunt his body holds. it frightens me.
the haunt his body holds. it frightens me. the haunt his body holds. it
frightens me. the haunt his body holds. it frightens me. the haunt his
body holds. it frightens me. the haunt his body holds. it frightens me.
the haunt his body holds. it frightens me. the haunt his body holds. it
frightens me. the haunt his body holds. it frightens me. the haunt his
body holds. it frightens me. the haunt his body holds. it frightens me.
the haunt his body holds. it frightens me. the haunt his body holds. it
frightens me. the haunt his body holds. it frightens me. the haunt his
body holds. it frightens me. the haunt his body holds. it frightens me.
the haunt his body holds. it frightens me. the haunt his body holds. it
frightens me. the haunt his body holds. it frightens me. the haunt his
body holds. it frightens me. the haunt his body holds. it frightens me.
the haunt his body holds. it frightens me. the haunt his body holds. it
frightens me. the haunt his body holds. it frightens me. the haunt his
body holds. it frightens me. the haunt his body holds. it frightens me.
the haunt his body holds. it frightens me. the haunt his body holds. it
frightens me. the haunt his body holds. it frightens me. the haunt his
body holds. it frightens me. the haunt his body holds. it frightens me.
the haunt his body holds. it frightens me. the haunt his body holds. it
frightens me. the haunt his body holds. it frightens me. the haunt his
body holds. it frightens me. the haunt his body holds. it frightens me.
the haunt his body holds. it frightens me. the haunt his body holds. it
frightens me. the haunt his body holds. it frightens me. the haunt his
body holds. it frightens me. the haunt his body holds. it frightens me.
the haunt his body holds. it frightens me. the haunt his body holds. it
frightens me. the haunt his body holds. it frightens me. the haunt his
body holds. it frightens me. the haunt his body holds. it frightens me.
the haunt his body holds. it frightens me. the haunt his body holds. it
frightens me. the haunt his body holds. it frightens me. the haunt his
body holds. it frightens me. the haunt his body holds. it frightens me.

the haunt his body holds. it frightens me. the haunt his body holds. it frightens me.

in bed listening to my love cry, waiting
for what will not come soon enough

from morphine pills, always waning
constipating his gut and mind, numbing mine

not to think table dust soap scum
must be something wrong with me

but then he quiets. be quiet! one moment
can't abide his moans and writhing

the haunt his body holds. it frightens me.

i've seen these white sheets
puffs of heaven in dreams
overlooking las vegas, god's chosen
city of my refuge this winter—
no shades or blinds to hide behind
inside a studio walled in gray
humming quiet. i see the storm;
it's not inside me. usually
i'm in the top fray like these
palm fronds wailing to deaf ears
on the other side of my glass window
view from common comfort felt
before by someone else
who ripped the duvet, but
that's okay because i am still
covered by the relief of not being
loved by friends who care
about what i don't feel like carrying
today, anymore, ever in my heart.
down comforter, help me rest.

if you see
millimeters rise
and fall above the torso
he's alive
if you hear
more than one final sigh
out the agape mouth
he's alive
if you feel
a slight cold
twitch of the foot
he's alive
if you smell
fear retreat
like a midnight shadow
he's alive
if you taste
salt seep along
your relaxed tongue

lord

off the tongue
like the first time a baby cries
like an alarm out of sleep
the end of a dream remembered again
in part, the rest of the words come
like a suckle on a breast cramps a womb
aching for the amen to come
like a belch in milky trance
after craving for a little, sedate
until hunger, nightmare, angry day
bring up unsettled food on the chest
off the tongue

lord

blood backwashes like tide dragging froth breathless
weights on hooks hang from clavicle and pocked lungs
when i'm happy. can you believe how
strange, how strain sneaks up on you

to think a back can carry, believe a fisted heart obeys
the will for eternity is heavy delusion
numbered eggs at birth, numbered beats at death
a valve unable to cover it all

sometime to be in comfort,
and sometime to fail and to be left

to themselves.
god willeth

we know he keepeth us [12]

peritonectomy with hipec
(flesh excavation and chemical flood)

> *nothing more can be done*
> said the doc, collective

sciatica and pinpoint pupils
(opioids are so unhelpful)

> *nothing more can be done*
> said the doc, collective

tangled web of tumors, nerves and organs
(an irradiated mess)

> *nothing more can be done*
> said the doc, collective

once a prophet raised a dead boy
(anyone?)

---

12   Julian of Norwich, Revelations of Divine Love, "The Seventh Revelation:
      Chapter XV"

a period of silence is kept

the people sit
his ear is a wide instrument
producing no sound, it measures
the timbre of painful memories
through thick fern overgrowth
hanging over the edge of his antitragus
otherwise, vibrations die at the roots

intercession is offered
her lower vermilion border bleeds jagged red
lipstick betrays contained, futile longing
for grandchildren, children, husband never had
time or peace to heal all these years
watching her beloved hibiscus pistils peak
and fail in every falling sun

the people kneel or stand
as she kneels and stands, her sheathed patellas do not ache
as much...*peace of the lord*...as her knuckles...*peace of the lord*...
when she pushes and pulls the mop stick clicking loose in its metal holding
polishing...*peace*...terracotta tiles, dusting chair pins, hanging curtains
the way her mother taught her...*how yuh do*...to do
for the rich people who live where bus doh run

all standing[13]

he depresses great and swell manuals together
with leather shoes lifting off the pedalboard
making hollow thuds beneath the bellowed creed
he plays with vigor as if it's his final crescendo
before his brow and type vii bald would be laid to rest
and no more sweat through kerchiefs and troubling nights alone

---

13   Taken from the rubrics of the Book of Common Prayer.

walled-in flower—
recite the office

of your dead
pale body of sin

reaching out the squint[15]
for the eucharist given

out another window
waste from daily bread

meted out guidance
from the third cathedral

view of your tomb
world forever behind stone

revelations of the divine
warm your withdrawn heart

surrounded by the same
sparse space and scarce feelings

comforted while tamping
your grave's earth

consider that lilies never work
like your calloused fingers

---

14 Julian of Norwich, Revelations of Divine Love, "The First Revelation:
Chapter VI"

15 A small window in an anchorhold where anchoresses like Julian of Norwich
could watch church services.

as discipline recommends
no admiration or holly beatings

just restraint
not to follow

pains in sorrow
suddenly giving way
to endless enjoyment

my heart, lord jesus
is a body part, not invisible
as my daughter thinks
it is, like her stomach
which makes me laugh
at the days to come—
what good is a cheerful heart
for his bones i see pressing
out of his skin closing
the gap to glory, hallelujah!

hurricane lamp smoldered
with fire-smoke making eyes
water in the glow rounding
out the darkness amplifying
the beating rain on the roof
seeping through to the tin pail
on the floor collecting water
shivering from being
a thing in the room, present
for questions while alone
while barricaded from flying
broken branches
flooding streets waiting to drag
downed power lines resting
like low swings near the sidewalk

god, are you hearing me?

cracks in gray pavement create
    room for grass to reach its broad sky

        a man's loafers sag at the insoles
            like his eyes at their inner canthus

dead palm fronds droop low
    unable to separate from their living core

        a woman's dry hair coils stand on end
            while she lingers beneath the falling trellis

the engraved *peace i leave with you*
    my peace i give you sanctifies the worn grain

        they walk by each other, exchanging
            footsteps, body scents and selfish deference

white stone hands, still moving
    still offering a gentle, pulsing holiness

        a white moth disturbed by a floating skirt
            ballooning around the knees, then falling

green canopy, tree bark, unknown fruit
    on the ground decaying to sprout and outlive

        clasped palms sweat, hanging over bent knees
            above loose gravel marked by restless shuffles

overgrown ivy blocking the beginning
    trail of a labyrinth path flanked by stones

---

16   Julian of Norwich, Revelations of Divine Love, "The Fourteenth Revelation: Chapter XLI"

glossolalia soft and loose on a tongue
in jesusname, jeeesusname

a lonely wooden cross withstanding
mist in the distance, heavy over the city

eyes catching, tracing small creatures
surviving without a prayer, thought of heaven

an old bell tolling for monks about their business
ritual welcome of souls seeking encounter

fix me
for my long, white robe [17]

---

17   "Fix Me, Jesus" is a popular African American Spiritual.

those robed footfalls
heavy with the dust of the same ground
caked with the mud of the slough, escaped
herded from every direction
to dip and wash hems
in red water

      a sign to those far from tribulation, far
      from the new cool of the day, far from
      never hunger or thirst
      never be stricken, never
      cry—
      can you see?

look up
clavicle the barre
for a long neck, craned

lean right
low towards the ground
summon, summon new life

lean left
low towards the ground
summon, summon the answer

stretch beyond reach
and run towards none
and fall into grace

be lifted and carried
placed on the same ground
to look up and stretch, low

whip the sky
fall away, whip
the sky that neither gives nor holds

be caught
left to pivot in stasis
and carried along the same ground[18]

---

18 Written to mimic the first 70 seconds of Alivin Ailey's "Fix Me Jesus"
    from Revelations.

fix me
for my starry crown

foreheads to vibrations in the sand
sticking to hair strands, old scalps

used to the contours of vibrato
brushing over backs, backsides and bare feet

as low as golden crowns placed away from—
in the space between christ's twisted thorns

and the kind of us
who crucified him

fix me
for my journey home

his soul's body lies in wait
to quake at the crossing

wooden cross hanging
from a loose black noose

a lighter burden.

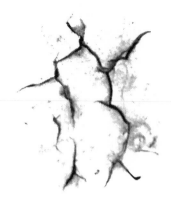